JUST FOR A THRILL

African American Life Series

A complete listing of the books in this series can be found online at http://wsupress.wayne.edu

Series Editors

JUST FOR A THRILL

Poems

Geoffrey Jacques

WAYNE STATE UNIVERSITY PRESS
DETROIT

09 08 07 06 5 4 3 2

Library of Congress Cataloging-in-Publication Data

Jacques, Geoffrey.
Just for a thrill : poems / Geoffrey Jacques.
p. cm. — (African American life series)
ISBN 0-8143-3290-0 (pbk. : alk. paper)
1. African Americans—Poetry. 2. Language and languages—Poetry. I. Title. II. Series.
PS3610.A35685J87 2005
811'.6—dc22

2005024940

Some of these poems were first published in the following periodicals: "Saturday Night Fish Fry," "Just for a Thrill," and "Bangs and Whimpers" first appeared in *Callaloo.* "James Baldwin" first appeared in *screens and tasted parallels.* "Inclusivity" first appeared in *O-Blek.* "Sunlit Frames," "Conditions of Artificial Scarcity," and "Nostalgia" first appeared in *Hambone.*

"Giant" and "The Blab of the Pave" first appeared in Melba Joyce Boyd and M. L. Liebler, eds., *Abandon Automobile: Detroit City Poetry 2001* (Wayne State University Press). The author gratefully acknowledges the generosity of the editors of these publications.

∞ The paper used in this publication meets the minimum requirements of the American National Standard for Information Sciences—Permanence of Paper for Printed Library Materials, ANSI Z39.48-1984.

For Lessie and Howard

CONTENTS

FOREWORD

Nathaniel Mackey

Geoffrey Jacques is a subtle, sophisticated poet who has read widely and has taken his cue from some of the most important vanguard poets of the past century and a half—Whitman, Breton, Césaire, Stein, Olson, Baraka, and others. He has digested and assimilated the lessons to be learned from their work while finding a way that is very much his own. The result is a distinctive contemporary voice whose angular mode of address and unerring touch edify as much as they impress.

This book presents both in full flower. Techniques of detour and indirection productively encounter an aesthetic of sampling, quotation, and juxtaposition, a language-foregrounding tack that draws a range of domains and discourses into its mix. Song titles, clichés, catch phrases, bureaucratic boilerplate, advertising jargon, office chat, song lyrics, legalese, and other components of the linguistic atmosphere we live in find their way into the work, suggesting an overmediated, gone-before-it-gets-here present. The poems, as oblique and understated as they are, convey a pervasive, abiding air of disaffection—even, without becoming strident, exasperation (quiet exasperation). Three lines of "Sepia-Toned Footage," for example: "sources: squid & lobster are spent / you couldn't pick a more meaningless measure / the undersigned, pursuant to said article." A distinctly musical yet astringent touch finds a place for randomness, whimsicality, caprice, non sequitur and such, a refusal to make what makes no sense make sense. Jacques' fleet, fugitive, anti-recuperative scat nonetheless appears intent on saying something about a numbing “universe of discourse,” at least on recontextualizing it. It’s to the work’s credit that we’re not quite sure whether this amounts to initiation or inoculation, making war or making peace with it.

Just for a Thrill is a substantial gathering of Jacques’ work of recent years—a welcome, breakthrough book by a poet whose work has appeared mainly in little magazines and limited chapbook editions over the past dozen or so years, a poet whose work deserves greater attention. We’re fortunate to have so galvanic a collection of Jacques’ poetry in an edition that promises to reach a wider audience.

I

SATURDAY NIGHT FISH FRY

lynchings have occurred because Negroes painted their
homes
aware of the scheme, some aides are told
—work out efficient behavior control techniques
this personal quality is ambivalent
there's no sign saying what they're made of—
black balls tilt under the red cap
years later the beatings continue

on a streetcorner way too far from Haiti
the drilling goes on into the night
lending the scene an elegant aura
the sweeping views will substantially change the
skyline

BURSTING OUT ALL OVER

who's got the night the right
way to say this edition's torn
but the reader's the comfortable one at the wobbly
  table
the precise consumption of crumbs
counts just like any corporate measure

again the night is potential robbery
a crime in the still dry layered air
a three-quartered disruption

none of these already-occurred instants
with the colors now arranged
like the whir of a clothes dryer keeping you at bay

but only a small adventure
its tiny events absent a story

INTRUSION

of a word or a set laid out here
no pot of gold must be tired
the only arrangement I know is
give me a cool drink of water

that's one name for a half-tone moment's air
& taken seriously the light turns suddenly
   citrus
its tubes uncovered when we stopped

a noise puts the face in your lap
the blond expired in the tunnel
you'll find part of it is but you've got to be
   patient
this island took some weeks to build

SEPIA-TONED FOOTAGE

will be out to force a public library
—balancing the budget—
including special building evictions

but you're still afraid
last frisked actually thanked him afterward
—market—
before, in the summer, plenty of others—

their street's really in a bad position
he says the bottom line right now
is unlike the United States
we don't have freedom
there's been a fundamental, systematic degradation
what we should do with all we have
or how to protect them

you've lived in New York for several years
we do sympathize
we're supporting them
we've got to have results from all this movement
sources: squid & lobster are spent
you couldn't pick a more meaningless measure
the undersigned, pursuant to said article

*

see the show—experience the dance
tickets to forever tango
will proceed a potent cold front: Concord
at the same time both have said they will do so

his last name's not mature enough to know your vast
experience
the hard-hat visit is a series for him
he clearly saw the commercial featuring the sepia-toned
footage
but five days may well agree with those words
which have considerably broadened his appeal

the consent orders—agreements with polluters
to change the report's methodology
—were deeply flawed
referring to the last time
no mention was made of a 17-minute speech
the city's greatest need is affordable housing
among gardeners, vacant lots

*

partly because of tightened space
we need a place like this
during a long workday they made Spanish cheese
& I love plants: humiliated, harshly rejecting
fluttering from the top: carelessly negligent & reckless

attach to the register to liquidate business: Connecticut
aggressive police tactics money & manpower
delivered toys & meals at Christmas
man beepers or check in by phone every time

—information—I am—I was—neighbors emerge—
pick them up in the afternoon
was discovered pointing to the window
exciting events without getting excited
& brought under ocher control

COMMERCIAL EUPHORIA

see it made: it's smart, it's simple, it's fast
Garner drops his chops in "street furniture"
the guy's mother's behind the wing
& strange-looking critters can't talk
—a very short fuse for psycho-ceramics—

*

commercial euphoria tracks gonads
the spills revert to weave: check your mailbox
white-shirt exit angular fixed rail
distort bins access recycled coverage
flashing crickets lead correspondence

*

it takes 30 years to learn
& I'm not sure I know it yet

dried coffee dribbles down the sculpted cup
like a shadow-rusted drainpipe
& the noise? here turning green
sounds far better than you remember
possum jumping the freeway
rabbits nibbling hotel debris
machines chattering along the grass

WHITE SUPREMACY IS NOT ETERNAL

alternatives to hegemony threaten certain interests
the dissolution of static notions has not kept pace
despite their final & well deserved death throes
the Nazis had a very tough position to sell
it was not a successful forum of a new type

the problem of white supremacy
is a multi-class phenomenon
because the United States is such a parochial country
—deeply inured, totally inane, totally absent of social context—
an intriguing metal masturbation multi-layered crisis

white supremacy is not eternal
is somebody smoking here?
a minor intervention a huge question
—stress on moralism—
patriarchal tribes invade matriarchal domains
we need to start interrogating this term "the west"!

think things through telescoped fashion
staggering knowledge, investment with no return
develop new language of analysis: state violence
  break faith—
where is the cohesion that pulls this thing together?
choose criteria that people have to meet

without taking into consideration
what is taking place in the world
give us an image of what we're after

*

something needs to be done
use hip-hop as an agent for social change
a plan of action going forward
an organized crisis
you've got to have the spin on it
you've got to have the sound bite on it

a tendency to streamline
a plurality of views & traditions
there are four planks to our platform
do we have fewer or many?
do we have our piece of paper?

*

we all know about that million thing
that doesn't preclude what people think
we're going to develop some more stuff
a one-page history: this process out off service

given the pre-established networks driving this
that's not something we can solve
with this temporary idea

who has the power to vote?
we don't know yet
the doors have to be open
you cannot have a biological test

AFTER MIDNIGHT

talk scares warm winds
—this should be comforting
& when they do, naturally, that flutter—

small gooey wheat odors
supplant normal city smells
& it's a good thing: the broken lamp brightens at the
   right moment
or the dying siren as you wake up

—he might just come to the door
& the broken shadow cross the threshold—

a pruned opportunity a jettisoned will

THE PRESENT "CRISIS"

A drat consequence. Volkswagens! Grooms stand for pumpkins, attitudes for wounds. Tree clichés forward my cubicles. Don't spill rants on the facial amber. It's smitten.

Slander grundy tastes like impulse yield. Knock that fox behind little worship. Notice? Gasoline. Let the green knives come closer: there, now we've got closure. No more chatty resistance to this spectacle. Evidence walks.

Zip your mouth, stand away from the hole. Advantage twin radiators, dust-rubber hearts; untie the slick gray trench. More information fabricates presentation, then stacks blue digit gavels. A marvel on the ground.

Roaring grub cracks star toothpicks. Pay the banana. Tease table sugar. Line the sidewalk with four films. Good Warnock, carelessly. String the pale palmettos. You've got the picture, now rest your weary saps on these mules.

STOMP

The parade is bound to get louder now
more insistent even as the ground rumbles
the choices left are the limited ones
a red sphere with its wrinkled face
the hole just left of the stem the sign that trespassing
   is spoken here
& if what looks green in this light
—as worn as everything here is it's hard to tell—
is at least unmarked, unwrinkled, well then—

*

our choices are sorrow the blues or pity
cross the street & try again

We took your side & argued till we were blue in the
face
as if that would've made you feel better about the whole
thing

Events might have turned out differently
but no one could compete with those cryptic messages

*

it's easy enough to make sense
call him a name & say it's an identification
use some tropes from old economics books
—who doesn't know them all by now—
as I think of you lying amid droppings & torn news-
  papers

*

truth is—as long as we consent—
we live in a democracy & can choose our tormentors
but none of those present asked for the broken promise
breaking through the still wind's veil

we can only aspire to imitate
the light at the bottom of a hill
where century-old houses feel
the earth's trembling sigh

*

the day we came to visit
one carried an ax another a lock & chain
four others hoisted a coffin
—our civilization—

the musicians didn't show
but there was lots of shouting & dancing
what else can you do after what's happened

*

no one mentioned you all afternoon
how you split without a proper good-bye
leaving us to explain everything
how a cipher greeted the ironic exhortation

it turns out no one heard us either
—who bore fresh figs & flowers on our visit—
the rain holding off as we wound through the streets
to our prearranged rendezvous
where we tried to be convincing

but it was as if a damp wind
took the music & spread it
like a sheet over the aging grass
our only comfort remaining the knowledge of your stilled
chatter

MESOPOTAMIA

everybody went crazy over the war
bodies shattering in the streets
strange utterances in the hallways
lovers abandoning each other among the ruins
children & calves born without skin ramble through the
  shadows
& faint cries in the rafters echo stillborn dreams

*

we lost each other the evening the bombs fell
a sun disappeared moments ago
its light unable to play in your fine hair
& in its absence agitated voices arise
—we've lost control our fantasies are becoming confused
there's too much pressure a voice raised in passion must be
   stilled
we must sacrifice love to the sounds of ghosts our eyes must
   not meet
our hands our bodies must not touch so often
& murderers suddenly appear over the wires, in our presence

*

& what if there had been light?
what's left behind is a digest of unshared moments
a trolley car in approaching spring
a brook emerging from a final dirty snow
a moment on the shore an ancient river
mountains exposing themselves in the azure mist

but no: in the end there was only a dream born without skin

*

either the dream or this burden haunts us now
all the smoke refuses to disperse
& the stench strangles the glitter from these self-congratulatory
exercises

this time it's hard to say where these lies leave us
alone & drugged in your tiny room
assuring yourself of victory
uncertain of the source of tomorrow's challenge
yet never wavering in the belief
that friends need to be told only what they're ready to
hear

& as we wait in the dark street trading tales of murderers
something precious is dying
& in the little window above a woman extinguishes the light

*

only recently we said each life was sacred
that our development would lead to your happiness

& a life by the sea a window open to the wind
was yours—& ours—for only the asking

but war arrived with its exposures & lies
with its sky choked by accusations
with its waters sullied by anxiety
& lovers were suddenly torn apart at the genitals

*

the smoke doesn't clear

the season of the cross the hour of ancient memories
the moment we realize what we've lost arrives
& in the midst of the charred corpses
of the blackened sky in flames
of an earth poisoned by infantile romances
an empty soul basks in the gritty afternoon
proclaiming once again its victory over the living

II

JAMES BALDWIN

there is a story here without names
like those who've never talked with you
& know all about you anyway
because in a city without alleys
little eyes never stop their curious wanderings
& sadnesses multiplied by sighs only a child can feel
flood these hopeless echoing streets

new names: Malcolm X Frederick Douglass Adam Powell
join the ranks of monuments
names grafted onto children a sign posting only our arrival
& the direction of yesterday's travels
the current shadows are themselves never given names
shielding a fear which stands in the light searching
for alleys here where I told you before
—mud puddles filled with reproducing sadnesses—

*

fire

each day we wonder when anger will once again arrive
& excuses become the dripping response to the sun in winter
an anger of living fire in the eyes of these young tenants
of cities mugged by their "betters"

anger instead of deadening silence
anger replacing ventilating hovels
anger pristine & dancing on the promenading tuxedos
anger devouring nests of caterpillar limousines
anger of the invisible suddenly arriving without announcement
anger of the unwanted guest at dinner
—this time come to stay—

anger stretching its arms its fists landing on diamond studded
  teeth
anger setting ivory & gold badges alight

while the next scheduled stop is announced on the loudspeaker

*

creationists

ashes brick mortar water song wood plaster cement words dance
chicken fried in the manner of the ancestors
glowing hordes of the blackest skins humans can produce
& these syncopated arms these arms!

this is our greeting our gift to tomorrow
all our masks thrown to the river
our smiles worn to please ourselves alone

WELL YOU NEEDN'T

you could find the shimmy
in sound & garlic, in green curtains
in mediocre speeches in faded magazines

waiting for the 8:30
the hazy Statue of Liberty streaks above cracked
 windows
up over the withered-winged yellow lights
in an old stick striking gold—

THE WONDERFUL FANTASIES OF THE COLONIZED

3 languages in 1 line followed by applause
a safari hat trotting down the avenue
a crack in the steamy hovering ceiling
I don't need a mirror, I've already got a self
if you don't like my peaches please don't shake my
   tree

I think it was sucking on all those lozenges
—quantity into quality—
additionally, we're trying to avoid the expensive
   paraphrase
critique of judgment: modernism
every kind of patch on my pants but a green-back dollar
   bill

if you don't like that version you can make up your own

GIANT

that day Johnson shot the man in cold blood
his bible & small frame house
just blending in with the crowd—
& when he saw his cousin cut in pieces
& strewn down a Mississippi road
he was five & vulnerable to several obstacles

out in leafy Auburn Hills
a guy got $46 million from the deal
—figuring by this proxy statement—
& expect no trouble: Mercedes won't stand
  contamination

most just want to keep coming every day
& his fast-talking lawyer said: *Walter P.*
& dammit we're still too close to see the thing
all this rot jamming the frequencies
15,000 hurt "& an unknown number dead"
sympathy grew when word got around

*

—just took things in his own hands—
a man & woman down already
it was just the fifteenth of July
& the tropical tomb's noise was deafening

I wonder if members got to vote
hear the whole deal's worth $36 billion
"the marriage partners differ starkly in culture"
& a whole generation of stupid ideas
lay shredding at the gilded altar

*

small producers must form their own alliances
"known for decades as ponderous,
slow-moving, intensely conservative"
—& as competition escalates
the marriage promises immediate access
without diluting the carefully cultivated upscale image—

we've got to burn off the modern grinder's rough edges
every shift the filters get clogged
& Ashlock picks up a pinion gear
& says he's going to smash Scott's brains out
& they went for an injunction & got it

—& the judge gave him $75 a week
retroactive to the day of the shooting—

THE BLAB OF THE PAVE

this is something besides a portrait
walls hum & drip on silver
metal quiet drapes dark floors

—he reads Adam Smith & is happy
to work 60 hours a week—

romantic fixations fall by the wayside
as her perfect sentences wax nostalgic

the visage rolls by like a train
balls of hay bouncing down the street
—you should have seen it—
the windows all lit & red toys on display

*

we talk about music
but not about TV
a cogent idea a bell instead of a buzzer

today K's mother-in-law
a cloth merchant from Dakar
stares across a plate of chickens wishing in
  Wolof

*

—well he'd better hurry
tell him he can take the freeway down—
with this weather he'd better be careful
—look just now for instance—
a pair of white eyes suddenly crowds out
   dreams
while you're splashing around
in front of that damned hospital
or along the school wall
ribs? who said ribs! one will be fine
you can't go east these days: it's blocked

*

all afternoon the mushy yellow rice
was the backdrop for our wandering
while yearning lurked beside the diverted glances
& everybody got suddenly busy
there go the bells & buzzers again
the cup's crumbs swirl endlessly
hours pass by & nobody notices

SUPPORTING ARCHITECTURE

supporting architecture is queasy
filling the platform with bundled stores
cobwebbed fences adjust leisure
packed desire bankrupting each claimant
the feature is you like it—don't you?—crumbs
  in your belt
strands of gray hair salt the totemized field

no I won't watch! zine-filled minds
develop saccharine revolts foggy zipless sex
—it's all smeared glass to me—
but this moves on despite the hour & its repetitions
so I've finally got to hand it to you: smashed corn
  turns white
& the gone gone one is its own slow rerun

JUST FOR A THRILL

it's not linguini or ice melting to the fridge's constant
hum

it's not an ironing board prop for a broken umbrella

it's not a boring video carted home in the rain

it's not your dirty bathtub

*

far be it from me to tell you how to spoke the hub

—continue your strong support
they're doing a remarkable job for us
if we don't act by April 29th
we'll lose the chance
to use all these challenges

we simply must find the will to pay our own way
it is possible to advance together across these kinds of
 differences
fueled by openness & promise

they like programs about chimps
like National Geographic specials
a lot of people are going to be hard put to explain why they're
 doing this
it's going to be an endless, ongoing activity
just an endless message from white America
it's balanced for a healthy diet

*

lingerie lotto live kiss
classical fascinating mystery:
of course the subject matters
a muse in Chicago unknown heroine—

*

on a concrete bench watching footfalls
she hears his unpleasant opinion made public
in a note written years later

but what listener knows the director's origin
footfalls never meant to be seen

*

nothing special I wanted to say
perhaps not so much as questions
it really is romantic if you think about it hard enough
but those involved lie on the narrative's margin

& who's got the nerve to question
this end-of-century model
its commanding synchronism, hissing & dripping

REVERIE

sitting here really is like eavesdropping
checking out clangs & chirps bouncing off bricks
rising above the commerce the green & yellow
   rustles

call it watching water boil
another summer's sweet silences
& that shimmering: "I love your body"
& there, I'll admit, the wrong message was taken
& infantile concerns along the map of milk

EVALUATION

neglects to respond altogether
it often takes months
for him to get out
after the holiday season

but no one outside the people knows
"I can't explain it: that's just the way industry is"
we paid the same amount buying the photo

business would know his job depends on doing it
  successfully
or question his pronouncements
that manipulation occurs on important issues seems
  insignificant
he'd be much more effective if he was honest & straight-
  forward

two other changes made to the text
how come there are no quotation marks

these are straw men

he blames the problem on being rushed
then reads two rooms
will ruin the aesthetics of the weight
work could be
where he wants to go
with what's present

*

make changes without consultation
& seem to care passionately
answer problems: “I have no idea how to do
others’ wishes & what he doesn’t want”
his response seems disingenuous
he doesn’t engender trust

he doesn’t follow the collective force
he has little or no respect

*

understanding & failure
remind repeatedly
not to follow-up on ideas

under supervision takes time to complete
& often don't get done at all
the result drags & we don't have a choice
the title word changes
to provide a (blank) to be consulted

low through assignments
here to decisions
take full responsibility

he blames a clash of cultures
he raises false issues

do we really want 18 words
believe we can call nature

*

it took months to get in
he especially avoids things he doesn't want to
  do

asserts common practice
seems to change to fit
what to do to hold on
because he's such a contrarian
he's often exasperating

*

you know you're right
at that point bold was removed
—marks were inserted—

the mailing problem couldn't identify
next day notice all openings
so delayed by the first week
despite GM intervention that cut
artificial distance a low productivity level

we have to indicate the data base
add a sentence (2 lines): "how can that be?"
many still hadn't received who was on what institutions
these problems were discussed

*

a trust problem claimed technical reasons
he was told work for him
or spend time supervising him
I don't consult the work of others

he defies wishes: "blows up"
demands reprints: despite his suggestion
his own request within several days
—& then told it was too late—

ad take those with ultimate control
he doesn't realize seriousness of issues or just doesn't
care
but wouldn't agree to sentence grammatical
even though the meaning & intent
conforms to his own judgment

*

especially egregious context suggests jargon laden
complicated nature of bulk trust
he should contact the lost post

does not follow up doesn't pay
didn't develop a happened to style
when confronted changes title

understanding procedures is off want
asserts things with such conviction
a bold tone an inappropriate indication

his response had no top attention
minute detail no apparent reason
pit bull determination entrepreneurial in December

he's not demonstrated significant change

III

THE CULTURE OF THE COPY

The prime rest of euphoria
The sinking lozenge of folders
The wrinkled rubber of paper
The counterweight of mailboxes
The paid pane of tasks
The gulping will of a lid
The falling exit that squeaks

The rind of talking
The question of hindmost
The tail of damping
The fern of allowance
The canal of need

Desire as sophistry
Lot as want
Temptation as production
Vomit as articulation
Hair as claim
Civilization as abuse
Agenda as packaging

Stark balls complete the referred pollen
Gasps of pleasure forbid mistakes
The greenhouse honors magnetic professions
Leaving social decisions prohibits anger
A catalogue of odors encases yellow cups

ONE YEAR LATER

the server's not working is just one phrase among
   many
we can curse them as much as we want
but nothing will return the lost marbles
or curb your fixation for yellowed paper

that last year still registers our letters
is something besides a neglected task
or a wrinkled plea to share your writing

I could ask if you'll ever face things
but why bother? at my back identical lights
   hover
& the quivering wheel stalls fear in the glass

LOOSE SENTENCES

that was your image lingering in the book
its coffee color its distilled odor
& now every sound galloping forward
reminds me how silence is really blue

like frosty corn kernels wasting away
or the burned-out hulk framed by azure molt
you now question how that place
came to drop those last digits

watching who balance the tracks
is one way that you're missing
that worthy twang those manners
it's contrition all over again

verses & tales on the grass in winter
is one way to go: but the moral
or whatever sense it made
urges a different bargain

DON'T BLAME ME

For Charlie Parker

How you can be o so misunderstood
no one wants your intention
but the clichéd story's real
& copies now clutter the ears in masked
   guitars

certain exits, of course, can't be helped
the whistle fails to drown
your pin-striped voice
now draped cleaner than a broke-dick dog
your techno-coated creation its baggy
   kinetics

AIMLESSLY ROAMING ALONG FIFTH AVENUE

a republic of the mind gone blank
air hums & leaks from the ceiling
the hand keeps slapping the number
its dim recess its corny irony
of course you know it happened again

from partying repeater-pencils she carries in
her lists
to infants vs. pedestals vs. exceptionals
let's find alternate yield signs
& applaud grinning starvation-mongers
their empty icy rattling cans
their warm tired wobbly plastids

decontrol is sticky-fudge seasonally adjusted
& toasty rolled at the ankles
like the old guys who meet again
to talk about wars dreams lost keys

WHAT I LEARNED

6 steps on the cracker jacks ladder
that's who's banging around this slushy morning
rustling bristles in the gray chirping winter
as he's so much later than normal

some keep little cards pinned with letters
or let the spillover trouble the neighborhood
but don't just sit in the middle: all gestures grant
   some shade
we're promised relief at last from the clouds
so bones in water can loosen long enough to move some
   dust around

HUMORESQUE

For Allen Ginsberg

I'm thinking about poetry a lot these days
strange intoxicant blindly spinning top
how wonderful to walk through Times Square
—your home now owned by Mickey Mouse—
& watch the merchants' verses fly through the
 sky

—nobody wants this useless toy—
a shallow brain's faint praise stares at your
 eyes

but there's so much more than skinny horny hips
shaking at the shiny night's joyful pricks & soggy
 tongues

three-quarters of a million sold
the world's gone mad! & the poem passes quicker than
 lust

SUNLIT FRAMES

—think of a purple shirt—
you can have the last word
the twenty-second letter
a somersault's extra faces

you're looking for... games confirm the stuff from
repro...

each task eats like celery
to arrive sometime soon

*

flatterers lick sunlit frames
perpetually suspended by chaos
starting at noon early liquids
lose their phytic touch

encourage all to get . . . debate empties the affirmed
 system . . .

rumors of tulips: a history
hang on for visual claims

*

the insulation's useless trope
returns diminished movement
voluntary spectacles fill papers
recycling self-purchased activity

someone figures here . . . classic unconscious avoidance
  maneuver. . .

drilling rattles the paved narrows
fritters away untapped enthusiasm

*

waiting bells could start immediately
ignore nouns until certainty erupts
knowledge hides behind each image
when fingers start a-popping

could be avoided... intends not to do much now that he
has...

memory calms jangling keys
your advice shorts the order

ROCK SERENITY

to say love even as we're trapped in grumpiness
such a corny thing this time of day
as hard city sounds rock serenity

& words float alongside corners of accidents & near
  misses

junk food philosophers unclaimed & unmatched
blurred exits indistinguishable chatter
clouded anxiety over time & desire

dare to say it all over again: stay by day
bowl of memory unscathed still-life nightlight
  parable

INCLUSIVITY

a few days ago a glimpsed river
became a lovely diversion from the room's smudged walls
its faces searching for a path to the cloud's horizon

you should know the difference by now
—how someone will let you peek into a hideaway
while your desire remains stubbornly elusive
& even though it resembles a performance
the distinction remains between memories—

like the way recycled ideas are appreciated
appearing like something we once owned
while around us erupt dreams of orange blossoms
& a shower of ready-to-eat raisins

*

searching in those out-of-the-way places is a mixed
  blessing
even though what's there once mattered
a day trip to the old whitewashed walls & gilded
  canyons
provides fewer answers than a marmalade jar
or a slight hint of morning haze
followed by afternoon sunshine with a chance of
  precipitation

*

so we return again to the two familiar rooms
where this tight-lipped bunch is admirably tolerant
   just as I am

& though I realized later that I needn't have dressed
it helped anyway—just as writing did—in putting the
   movie together
it also helped that someone liked
the names dropped in the course of the morning

NIGHT LANGUAGE

listening to Jayne Cortez

—everywhere the cinnamon topaz flea bites
exhibit humidors of benzene pigeon indexes pulsing with
  iodine honeydew
roaring hummingbirds spit in the lake

fluttering financial astronomers gyrate
to the unnatural holler of stuffed animals

circumcised bumblebees ritual wax supermarkets
live filthy clay cheek peanut intensities
voltages of hollow monkeys of frozen insults & cyclone
  meditations
forgotten mercenary clerks
wooden mute suns sanitized lollipop tangerines
& compressed numbly ripped matter escape the scorched
  telephone
bleeding quinine bellies dislocate tremors
catacombed pigeon moans
mate in alert pearly eyed windows—

AMUSEMENT WITHOUT WEATHER

calmly take the object out of the water
one is blue, so much like its casing
life here engages atrophied elephants

we've just arrived but the crowds are leaving
displaying honored fidelity to ancient custom
words break along the trestle like a pair of shoes on
marble
their flaky buzz, their pink, rolling ball

AT THE BORDER TO THE UNEXCEPTIONAL SKY

the rugged moon tears away
from its radiant housing
above the lonely garages

as if doing just that
was sufficient tonic
a good enough barrier
an acceptable excuse with strength to soothe the
blues

the scavenger's revenge
is like the cool autumn palette
an orange-spurting sound

*

as he goes on about missed appointments & lost
  language
the rough disk of nocturnal light
like this pair of lovers
rcminds him smiling now
of what's heard in dreams
of shouts thrown at the sky

*

remember when the lollipops died

—& someone else knew the drama
traveled by the mind's complex passions—

trains speed past in a blur
the luminous blue & amber
melt together in unbroken intimacy

I'll learn nothing here
my eyes fastened to the floor
my rhythmic heels drowned by machines

while in this vacant space
objects lose their crisp lines
their host a ruptured warren

SIX EPISODES IN THE HISTORY OF FLIGHT

for example: the drenched air's muted calls
sparse reminders of an unkept promise
of the starving clinging to gutters
—no it's not, the fact was announced yesterday—
the chance of clearing by afternoon

*

here's where the best intentions fail
all he wanted was peaceful prosperity
the news brought instead a platter of slaughtered
  pigeons
our calling now is to pick up the pieces

*

it's a hell of a job a golden opportunity
I keep waiting for you to show up
the revolution arrived in the mail
an official let the truth slip out then took it back
amid groans from the mechanical recorders

*

the scribe said: this actually happened
then went on to other ideas
what's missing is love's fine odor

but maybe we're expecting too much
from those not grown enough to know their own
minds

*

at least the crime novels will get better
household help will get cheaper
who won't do anything for a buck
now it takes about ten
thc kids don't mow lawns
machines & strong men hum in the suburbs

*

the upper mouth remains rancid
they all gathered in the capitol for prayer
a few days later the lawmakers voted
to sacrifice the nation's children
find the missing letter here

NOTICE

stop cuts wages war service
the official election is disabled
we want your option the more controversial the
  better

look around folks—you'll see it everywhere—
you're being reconfigured restructured downsized
the remaining shift gets the shaft!
do you have adequate security?
tell us how you'll be reached

we're concerned about senselessness
automatic weapons like the one shown above with
  appropriate exceptions
state auction is particularly crucial
give us your reports complaints compliments anecdotes

BANGS & WHIMPERS

the guy must have been tone deaf
heart dead as a doornail
that wasn't just some numb thud
spin around toward the cracked mirror
could be your moment calling like a gaseous
   zebra
or a metal cloud passing through the stands

he says he wants seafood
hold tight! the woman at the microphone
is counting the tide's footprints
the fuzzy coverlet keeps the gull's sound
   muffled
an echo like elephant patter

IV

THE FALL OF VIETNAM

the mountain goats of Montana shed their coats
good for the mountain goats of Montana

the symbol of our presence in Vietnam
—if we can't prevent the Embassy from being captured
by God what are we there for—

the faded whites of their wedding gowns
is that the right number? a ticklish subject
—design writing research—
"the learned & affable meeting of frequent academies"
& some fatty sweat for you

I could sit through all your lies missing you
—but I still don't have a good hat—

*

“I wanna be vamped by you just you
& nobody else but you”
that’s not quite right: kill the flies
then change the stinking yellow pillowcase

I don’t have $100 to be dropping on forty minutes
my hunch is it’s a gateway thing

thirteen months fourteen days $300 million a day
“do you remember, will you return”
we never did get the two Hueys straight

what I most want is people arguing on the sidewalk

THRENODY FOR EDSEL REID

Work with extreme randomness
welcome to the house of fame
—no one among us wants it like this—
all this constant toing & froing

October *is* twilight: time's loss
shifting colors mysterious knocking
—this constant humming in the ears—
you can't hear it? no, I suppose

those swans nearby hover aimlessly
a tribute, a warning, a greeting, even
—what's left are old phrases: supreme,
to say, the voyage, a dancing dolphin

CONDITIONS OF ARTIFICIAL SCARCITY

a very strong but limited boundary
an isolate (what's the word?) obliterates!
—lives somewhere with someone who also lives somewhere
 & returns to the somewhere where they were living—

sees the force as essentially disappearable
its points of origin explicitly theorized in conditions of
  artificial scarcity
alongside the impulse to redistribute

*

now the war has "ended"
there is no clarity
victory: something vile in nature
inherent wickedness is not pressured

sleepless shadows pull the doll apart
in an oddly familiar demobilization which cannot be
cured
abandon all interest in the present & the future

egos demand adaption at all costs: multiple collections
the facts in dispute—screen memories not usefulness—
the object can be repaired time & time again
what is certain is the need for heroism

*

1. The forty-year war.

2. Two hundred & fifty thousand dead.

3. Seventy thousand amputees.

4. Two million land mines.

5. Lost limbs? None for you.

*

everyone is subject to an increase or a decrease of these
forces

proper rituals must be accomplished

the integrative events are very close

your English is excellent

we don't talk about unknown things

the problem of pre-figuration

NOSTALGIA

> "[A]esthetics is for me what ornithology must
> be for the birds."—Barnett Newman

If you could see me now
—after I've spent the night frolicking
you'd laugh, you'd cry, whatever—
& no this sack's not gone awry
it's still waiting for your big hands

*

rose bush rose bush rose bush red
what's the difference between your name & the
poem?
call it film noir call it candy
dozens went the way of the format

*

say it's wonderful so wonderful
it's a shame you'll never complain again
—as I was saying before I was saying—
we could *study* clichés but there's no fun in
that
better to go to bed & stare at the sickle moon

*

where angels fear to tread
one of us will stand & catch the 7:30
& then? exhaustion produces sharp multiple
 particles
the small price fascinates

*

the month will be "May" for awhile
but with all this heat we're having you'd almost
 wish
for a different, truer knowledge
—an essentially fashioned blindness, for instance

*

sweet comic buds soaked nearby
the form the utterance sliced in half
—this time the dream's a rouge veranda—
& word comes a few weeks later
after the ore cools down

*

who kissed in a field of white?
this family tree's association is crowded
violets are passionately cybernetic
—as if that were still the standard attack—
& the dismissals trivialize authoritarianism

*

when you open it to speak are you:
—about that plate & gravy—
drilling for scholars, dialing for…?
questions of fanaticism
questions of colonialism

*

when will they ever learn
the traditional sources have been scooped up
another one walks this way: "I'm a court jester"
naughty heat is something good
just move to where you'll see more

*

awaken with the sun & order orange juice
for one stuffed chocolate bear
one soaked hand one pile of streaked dust
purple-sprinkled hair spotted under the just-shined
  lights—

*

go swinging low bye-bye
& take that gruff snot with you
read that ancient narrative the slave's old poems
think & write a paragraph:
"I laughed when I heard you say..."

*

these arms about you
that'd be nice: many charms have been laid
—let's not go there now—
the raft on the bank is well hidden
—let's get back to work—

*

these lyrics this language its rhythm a syntax of
evaporations
of deferrals of concupiscent exclamations
a nightingale sings: con alma
& is never in this chorus forgotten

*

the start of a summer night: blue
are you interested? or can't you just
look without thinking about that phone call & its
consequences—
it don't mean a thing, all you got to do—

*

she's a fine old hoochie-coocher
but brittle every step of the way
slick & fried & wrapped tight as a spool
the shining ochre window calls:
so generally acceptable a code is steamy

*

never tell me dreams come true
I know them as fetishes
come to chase away discolored leaves
—the lies they tell! the corroded oil pipes!
those fading morning sirens! the dust!

*

I was thinking about interest
—is you is or is you ain't—
but the razzle-dazzle got to me
& things just got to happening
—at the window, the stick started swaying—

LETTER TO THE BOARD

I

We've asked for their response. Name names. Say he's been hired. It should be on paper. We've got the next meeting. Something about designer progress. And what about the conference? I'll stick to my original idea: tall wind. A little more provocative. Between crevice and sand, the longer we wait, the less likely we'll meld.

II

The letter could be ready after index. We've not as a three-headed beast. You really want to look left in a very weird way. My gut tells me they're just tremendous, they're luminous. Change the title, finalize. I was just passing information. I'm getting reimbursed. It would have cured what ailed you. March fell into the exchange.

III

Could've been faxed that. Get a call back number. She just walked in. For shouting among bank education, the shadow's pulse is fired at the cabin. A caution in no way complete met established criteria, hosted by the roots. The numbers creating this perception are pretty impressive. Gains exceeded 20%; half are from outside.

IV

Reflectors tend to be self-regulating, referring to industries later covered up or torn down. They've become social artifacts, mindlessly fueling expansion, an exuberant, pastoral sanction. Absent a barbed-wire wall, begin weaving. Impact distribution and promotions. Sulfur of sneers, date of fellowship, that's another thing.

V

Only thing I don't like, they don't put sauce on them. Excuse B and C. "This kind of bird is a boodge." It's quiet, a little fizz from that side. I never know when the explosion is scheduled. Schedule the put-down out, like bad air. The window is not open. Take great care to ensure only those who qualify receive them. A misnomer forages.

VI

Our agreement should be as binding as one's word. You have to hope it's not repeated everywhere. Create warm, fuzzy feelings, continue with an image campaign. No problem. Sheer survival is a big part of our embrace. The drawdown was smaller than expected: committed, approved for short-term use related to engineering.

VII

I can't come to the phone right now. It's hard to understand how you can even think that way, the queasy feeling of a solid bond having been shattered. The best-intentioned flub it. Her range of forecasts is quite wide. Expecting a rise this year but surprised at the surge. Reaching this milestone means fortunes are glistening.

VIII

Experts say the punitive damages are excessive. Who elected them? Affix your validation. From now on, you'll be twice liable, slightly less than expected. Traditional performance measures have been warning for some time that the items have gotten too expensive. Strong sectors include technology. Narrow leadership is optimistic.

IX

Consumers have suddenly "got religion," and pressures are boiling over their buying proclivities. It's no fun to be on the wrong side of the train. Given these strong flows, it's anybody's guess: not many are further out. Just one of the crystal ball gazing analysts is defiant. On a pro forma basis, comfort perennially confounds the bulls.

X

You won't notice a thing. Their posture has reinforced long-standing tensions. This is total boilerplate. I was stomping around here for weeks, very unproductive and confused. Our board did not arrive here until Tuesday night. It isn't that I'm not working; we'll take any donations. Members pilloried by critics, the data raises new doubts.

XI

We saw each other briefly, without speaking. About passengers, I don't know. There needs to be dredging. The same word is used interchangeably for two different things. You have to blast the rock out of the way. It is an enviable—and excruciating—position, how you can serve the thousands of simultaneous connections.

XII

I don't know that I'm at liberty. Especially for the Brazilian, who has transformed our future path. I appreciate knowing you might be targets for the exercise. Her success isn't startling: she's the linchpin for one of the biggest coups ever. It highlights a contradiction at the heart of advertising: the consumer is not a moron.

XIII

This is an update. The headache of the moment has become a place to borrow. Today's report put a fresh face on the problem. This is the wild card: planners and leaders are playing catch-up in a big way. Borders are bottlenecks where shipments must be hauled off. There are three widths. In a number of cases, they are opening the door.

XIV

The successors are searching for a new mandate. The whole administration has changed. In total, it wasn't a basket case. We're using intermodal wherever it's expedient. For all this, movement won't come smoothly. Take a page from across the Atlantic. An agonizing decision, with small market share and a mountain of debt.

XV

The firm often throws out old equipment. They're very territorial and won't give out the number. He has to keep working or he'll drown in data. Russian academics recently did *Webster's Unabridged Dictionary* by hand. I just sprout legs and run. But not the whole picture: the archives are mirrored on hundreds of sites worldwide.

XVI

A foundation is mad. You can't rush panorama. Bring me the sour plaza. I'll just stop back by. Who's got time to come back to this. It all boils down. Your responsibility spends all the time sleeping off the proper care and feeding of bread. Those random suppressant particulars. Now we can keep you agitated. This demands a call.

XVII

Gut feelings are tracked to the source. If things are good, it must be time to split, suggesting that the event is meaningless. I find the norm is absolutely no service. Somehow its noisy, nutty, anarchic spirit was well represented by a 40-foot iguana on the roof. I was presold. The themes quickly become established as true.

XVIII

Fiscal fandango damages an emerging harassment. A month ago both began complaining about offensive remarks. It had nothing to do with race. The remedy is to simply stop talking about it. He responded to the valuations, which understates inflation. Pass go, collect cheap burgers, narrow the current account deficit.

XIX

Don't worry about Miriam's. Hers is the 26th, I think. A labyrinth of luck, when warnings are intelligent, appropriate and useful. The sticker on an aluminum stepladder is nearly a foot long. How much to put that label there. People get really worked up. It's fun! But the question of "post-sale duty to warn" has not yet been decided.

XX

Rules on options could alter perception. It's not a perfect world, so we'll do what it takes to keep it interesting. You don't really need two voices: she stepped out. Anybody got the order sheet? Tell you what. She was going to work Friday. We can trace any growth to improved circulation. Most space holds empty equipment.

XXI

There's no rush, he's asleep. It's quiet. We'll try to get it done by the end of the day. But you can't copy. Thank you. I'm sorry to bother you. He's got his hat and his apple. You've a history of more pessimism than turned out. We just hope correction gets factored in. They come down to something more normal. Security flaw.

XXII

It never needs a battery. This research generates social empathy. There's no difference between what she sells and who she is. An entire city is on alert. But we feel one way at the beginning and another way at the end. It passed on the representation. A perfect collection for today's malady: margin for error, demand volume discounts, secure united rule, admit ideal powers.

XXIII

We should set up for tomorrow today. I know you barely have time to do the laundry. Because I am at it again poking into your future plans. We don't give up and don't want you to either. I've since added a few things along the way, while these defensive folks try to figure out how we keep this thing afloat that's steadily declining.

XXIV

They underestimate themselves. We want to be at the table at this point. My hope is in that amorphous thing we can begin to shape forms. Sounds broader than it is. This thing impinges on me. It connects to folks who probably defend social legislation. You'll get the card next week. Readers are interested in you. Take a walk.

XXV

Was there ever any feedback? Tell me your fantasy. Your job is to figure out how to make it work. All of it works on our external face. You get the picture. You can push those same kind of tensions onto the national scene. We're too fragmented to be effective as a challenge. While you are out, construct another place to go.

XXVI

His assistants may have contributed to them, but big hurdles remain. You are going to see some very interesting alliances evolve. Regulators are expected to give qualified approval. That prompted a last minute blast of criticism, so the letters exited. We are very interested in their premise. Cheap long distance, final revisions slow the pace of loss. Please explain.

XXVII

They should contextualize their figures. I'll hear a single tone, then the "camp-on" light will flash. An idea that lends depth to the issue. Telecommunications. Theorists gnaw on the issue, due in the fall, of unparalleled abundance. Rather than citing another study, slaughter alternatives. "Road kill on the information highway" improves output.